MW00355076

small woodturning projects

with Bonnie Klein

12 Skill-Building Designs

FOX CHAPEL
PUBLISHING

© 2005, 2013 by Bonnie Klein and Fox Chapel Publishing Company, Inc., East Petersburg, PA.

Small Woodturning Projects with Bonnie Klein (ISBN 978-1-56523-804-6, 2013) is a revised edition of *Classic Woodturning Projects with Bonnie Klein* (ISBN 978-1-56523-260-0, 2005), published by Fox Chapel Publishing Company, Inc. The patterns contained herein are copyrighted by the author. Readers may make copies of these patterns for personal use. The patterns themselves, however, are not to be duplicated for resale or distribution under any circumstances. Any such copying is a violation of copyright law.

Interior photography by Bonnie Klein and Greg Heisey.

ISBN 978-1-56523-804-6

Library of Congress Cataloging-in-Publication Data

Klein, Bonnie.
  [Classic woodturning projects with Bonnie Klein]
  Small woodturning projects with Bonnie Klein / Bonnie Klein.
     pages cm
  Originally published as: Classic woodturning projects with Bonnie Klein, 2005.
  ISBN 978-1-56523-804-6
  1. Turning (Lathe work) 2. Woodwork. 3. Woodwork--Patterns. I. Title.
  TT201.K56 2013
  684'.08--dc23
                          2013008593

To learn more about the other great books from Fox Chapel Publishing, or to find a retailer near you, call toll-free 800-457-9112 or visit us at *www.FoxChapelPublishing.com*.

Note to Authors: We are always looking for talented authors to write new books. Please send a brief letter describing your idea to Acquisition Editor, 1970 Broad Street, East Petersburg, PA 17520.

Printed in China
First printing

Because working with wood and other materials inherently includes the risk of injury and damage, this book cannot guarantee that creating the projects in this book is safe for everyone. For this reason, this book is sold without warranties or guarantees of any kind, expressed or implied, and the publisher and the author disclaim any liability for any injuries, losses, or damages caused in any way by the content of this book or the reader's use of the tools needed to complete the projects presented here. The publisher and the author urge all readers to thoroughly review each project and to understand the use of all tools before beginning any project.

Bonnie Klein

When Bonnie Klein discovered woodturning, it became an obsession that has not gone away. It all started with the purchase of a Shopsmith lathe because her daughter wanted a doll house. During the process of building, lighting, and furnishing, Bonnie became mostly interested in the tools, an interest that may have come from her father, who was a builder. Nearly 20 years ago, Bonnie designed and began producing a small woodturning lathe. The development of the Klein lathe was a new beginning for what she likes to call "small scale" turning. For this reason, most of her turnings could fit into the palm of your hand.

Since the early 80s, she has attended most of the major woodturning symposiums in the U.S., sometimes as an attendee, but many times as a demonstrator. In addition to the many teaching venues around the U.S., Bonnie has also traveled to Australia, New Zealand, Ireland, England, France, and Canada to teach and demonstrate.

Bonnie particularly enjoys working with young people and getting them excited about woodturning. Because sharing her passion is something she feels strongly about, Bonnie has volunteered many hours of teaching and sharing woodturning with kids.

In addition to turning and teaching, Bonnie has served on the board of the American Association of Woodturners for six years; for five of those years she was vice-president and conference coordinator. In 2003, the American Association of Woodturners recognized her with an Honorary Lifetime Membership for her contributions to woodturning.

Bonnie's work has been featured in *American Woodturner*, *Woodturning (UK)*, *Woodwork*, *American Woodworker*, *Wood Magazine*, *Fine Woodworking*, and in many books. For more information on Bonnie and her work, visit her website at **www.bonnieklein.com.**

Acknowledgments

I would like to acknowledge a few good friends who were very influential early in my woodturning career. I received my first formal woodturning instruction from Denver Ulery. I learned so much from Wally Dickerman, who was part of our woodturning club in the very beginning. I must credit Dale Nish for literally pushing me out in front of an audience and starting me on the road to teaching and demonstrating. Anker Rasmussen built a lathe for me, which later became known as the Klein Lathe. Much of the foundation of my woodturning skills as well as my teaching and demonstrating abilities, I owe to the guidance and support of Richard Raffan and Ray Key.

Most of all, I would like to acknowledge my husband, Robert, for his patience and support and especially for the fact that he never complains about my heavy tool boxes.

I'm indebted to these people in addition to so many others in the woodturning community I have had the good fortune to learn from and associate with so far in my career.

Foreword

"Just one more thing," Bonnie said at 2:30 a.m. I met Bonnie Klein in Lexington, Kentucky, in 1987 at the first American Association of Woodturners symposium. We became good friends, roomed together many times at future symposiums and other woodturning events, and would talk about woodturning into the wee hours of the morning. Since then, our love of woodturning has taken each of us in many directions. Bonnie has taught and demonstrated over the years, and she has a special place in her heart for students. She has taught classes for many girl scout and boy scout troops, for 4-H clubs, and for home schooled children as young as six years old. Bonnie motivated students in her classes and made woodturning fun. She creates a very relaxed atmosphere that puts students at ease.

Bonnie is fascinated by many different aspects of the turning field. She began turning on a wood lathe and eventually bought an ornamental lathe. She also learned metal spinning. Known for the diversity of her work, Bonnie uses many different materials and creates unique effects with the use of color on her turnings. I remember a piece I was especially fascinated by: a set of seven threaded nesting boxes turned out of blackwood. Her level of craftsmanship was excellent. She has also made a turned and carved chess set. In the last several years, Bonnie has

collaborated with other woodturners in the field, and she is known for her threaded spin top boxes. Upon opening the spin top box, you will find a treasure inside of one or more miniature tops.

I see a bright future for woodturning. Numerous scholarships have been awarded by the American Association of Woodturners to start woodturning programs across the country. There are many individuals and local chapters sponsoring woodturning classes in schools for students of all ages. With the help of teachers like Bonnie, woodturning will continue to grow and provide many hours of satisfaction to woodturners around the world.

I'm sure you will enjoy the projects in this book as much as I have and also create some new projects of your own. I'll always remember Bonnie saying how fascinated she was by watching an object emerge from a piece of wood. It was like magic how a piece appeared before your eyes. So. . . go to your shop, turn often, teach your daughter, son, or grandchild to turn wood, turn safely so you can enjoy it for many years to come, and, remember, there are many ways to learn, and one of the most gratifying is to share your knowledge with others.

Mary Lacer
Former Executive Director
American Association of Woodturners

Table of Contents

Woodturning Basics
7

Acorn Box
16

Carrot Pen
23

Sunburst Earrings
26

Resources
72

Spiral Chatter Eggs
32

Letter Opener
36

Stir Fry Spatula
42

Spin Top
46

Tool Handle
50

Whistle
54

Yo-Yo
59

Honey (Bee) Dipper
64

Purse Mirror
67

Introduction

This is not a "how-to-turn" book, but more like a "recipe" book. It also isn't a coffee-table book, so take it with you to your workbench.

This book is written assuming that you have the knowledge and skills to accomplish basic woodturning. Each project has been photographed step-by-step and is accompanied by instructions. The projects have been selected to demonstrate a wide variety of techniques and decorative enhancements. Each one has a little something beyond the ordinary and is a learning experience in itself. By mastering the individual techniques, you will add significantly to your woodturning repertoire. Any one of these projects would be perfect for a parent (or grandparent) to use to introduce a child (or grandchild) to woodturning or for woodshop classes, 4-H clubs, scout gatherings, and so on.

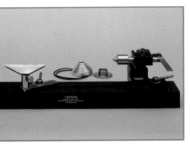

Klein lathe

The wood used for the projects throughout this book is *Acer saccharum* (sugar maple or rock maple), an excellent wood for turning. I have chosen this maple for several reasons. The light-colored wood is easy to photograph, thereby better illustrating the processes. One of my goals was to give a uniform look to the projects by using a rather plain wood, making it easier to demonstrate the enhancements and special techniques. A plain wood is good for practice, and it leaves room for inspiration. With this maple, there are no problems with grain density or openness. When you make a good cut, it shows. Sugar maple, often in the form of 2"-diameter dowels, is my wood of choice whenever I teach or demonstrate.

Another one of my goals was to minimize the equipment and tools needed to accomplish these exercises. The only lathe tools used for the turnings in this book are a ⅜" shallow fluted gouge (spindle gouge), a parting tool, a ½" round

nose scraper, a ¼" square nose scraper, and a ½" skew chisel. It is not necessary to use the exact tools that I have chosen; make your tool selections based on your own preferences. In addition to the lathe, a fairly essential shop tool is the band saw. All of the turnings are done either between centers or mounted on a faceplate. There are no three-jaw or four-jaw chucks used for the turnings in this book. Because most of these projects have a diameter of less than two inches, they can be turned at speeds up to 3,000 rpm. Spinning a chuck in this speed range is a safety hazard, and the body and jaws often limit tool access around the workpiece.

I like the idea of making your lathe work for you. For the variety of projects in this book, the lathe will become a disc sander, a buffing machine, and a horizontal drill press.

Although they could be done on any size lathe, these projects lend themselves to smaller lathes. The techniques and cutting theory are the same for any size lathe, but smaller lathes are quieter, require less shop space, and, for many, are less intimidating than a larger machine.

All of the projects in this book have been done on the Klein Lathe, which I designed and have been producing since 1986. My small lathe was part of the beginning of a new era of modern woodturning with tools, kits, organizations, books and videos, gallery shows, and eventually many small, imported lathes.

It is my hope that as you work (and play) through each of the projects in this book, your skills will improve, your woodturning enjoyment will increase, and you will be inspired to continue practicing, experimenting, and learning.

I turn for the love of the creative process. I am addicted to discovery, progress, and the fact that perfection is forever elusive, but as I strive for it, yesterday's challenges become the basic skills of tomorrow.

Happy Turning,
Bonnie

Woodturning Basics

As I mentioned earlier, this book is not designed to be a "how to turn" book; rather, it is meant to add to your toolbox of woodturning skills, projects, and techniques. The following chapter covers techniques for preparing a glue block to mount your work on the lathe, for burning lines, for creating several types of chatterwork, and for finishing. The finishing methods presented in this book have been well tested in many demonstrations and workshops. However, I would like to point out that finishing for "gallery quality" turnings would typically involve greater attention to the sanding process and possibly other finishing products.

Read these sections before you begin, so that you can become familiar with the skills. Then, refer back to this chapter for the details needed to perform the specific tasks for each project.

The wooden tool models shown here are much larger than life size and are used in demonstrations and workshops as aids when describing the tool shape or a cutting technique or when discussing the bevel. These wooden models travel with me wherever I teach. I must give credit to my friend Del Stubbs for this idea.

For more information about shaping, sharpening, and using these specific tools, I suggest watching the AAW video *Fundamentals of Sharpening*.

These two wooden models show the shapes I prefer for my round nose and square scrapers. Both are sharpened on the end and along the left side. On the square scraper, the angle at the corner where the side meets the end should be less than 90 degrees.

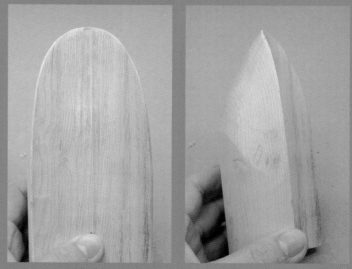

The basic ⅜" spindle gouge is one of my favorite turning tools for the projects in this book. It is a shallow-fluted gouge, sometimes nicknamed a "fingernail gouge" because of its shape. It should have a smoothly curved cutting edge, and I prefer an angle of 35 degrees for a good functional tool.

Glue Block Preparation

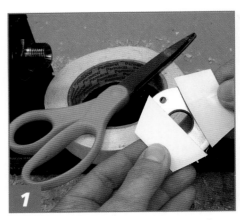

1

Cut pieces of double-faced tape and attach them to your faceplate.

A few of the projects in this book will be mounted on a glue block. There are several reasons why this is good practice. For small scale projects spinning at higher speeds, it is safer (for your fingers) than using a three- or four-jaw chuck, and you will have better tool access to the back side of your work.

The glue block (also known as a waste block) is attached to a faceplate and becomes a convenient mounting surface for your turnings. To prepare your own glue block, follow the step-by-step photographs shown in this section. My wood of choice is ¾"-thick pine cut to the size of the faceplate and attached with double-faced, pressure-sensitive tape. My glue of choice is medium or thick cyanoacrylate glue used with an accelerator.

With this type of mounting, the workpiece is held securely until you are ready to part it off. You don't have to worry about running your tools into screws, and the blocks can be reused many times, until they are about ⅛" thick. To replace them, just turn away the wood, peel off the tape, and start over. (Caution: Heat will relax the grip of the tape. If your headstock bearings run warm, they may also warm up the faceplate, thus causing the tape to loosen. The solution is to use screws or to adjust the tension on your bearings.)

2

Before peeling off the paper, cut off the excess tape.

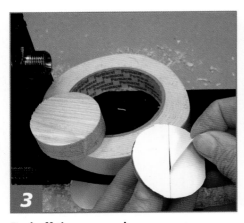

3

Peel off the paper when you are ready to attach a glue block.

4

Press the glue block onto the tape, and then clamp firmly in a vise for about 15 minutes. This is pressure-sensitive tape and must be clamped for strength. It may be good to reclamp the glue blocks occasionally.

True up the sides.

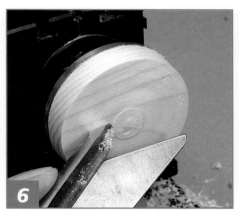

Flatten the face after adjusting your tool rest to support the tool for the entire cut.

Until you gain the expertise with the gouge to make the surface flat enough for a glue joint, you could do some leveling with the skew chisel lying flat on the tool rest. Keep practicing with the gouge.

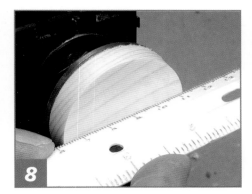

With the lathe off, check to see that your surface is flat.

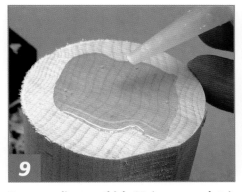

Use a medium or thick CA (cyanoacrylate) glue on one piece of wood and spray the accelerator on the other piece.

Put the two together and hold for a few seconds until the glue sets. Before turning the lathe on, spray some accelerator on any glue that squeezed out.

True up the sides in preparation for turning a project.

Burned Lines

A burned line is a simple detail that can be used to set off chatterwork or to accent colored areas. If the workpiece is small in diameter, you will need to speed up the lathe to build the heat more quickly. Stainless wire works best and is readily available as fishing leader. Using paper to burn lines gives you the opportunity to burn some lines on other surfaces of your turnings.

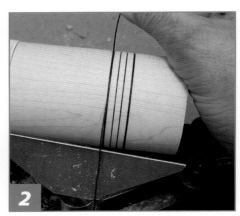

1 On a practice piece of wood, use the tip of a skew lying on its side to make a few grooves.

2 The two outer lines have been burned with a heavier gauge wire—about 18g. This wire is stainless steel and won't anneal and break when it gets hot.

3 The two inner lines have been burned with a finer gauge wire—about 22g. Hold the wire against the piece without moving it back and forth.

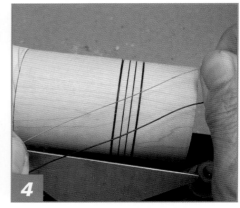

4 Here is a comparison of two different wire sizes. Experiment with other sizes.

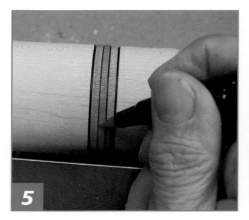

5 The burned lines help to accent the colors.

6 If you would like to burn a line on the face of a turning, first make a small groove with the tip of the skew lying flat on the tool rest.

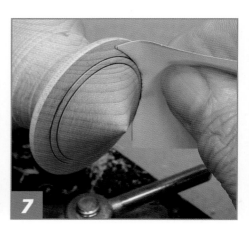

7 Use a piece of paper—20 lb or 24 lb—held in the groove until it burns. You will need to speed up the lathe and will know it is working when you see smoke. Heavier paper will be better for burning lines in larger grooves.

Chatterwork

Chatterwork is the texture created on your workpiece when either the tool moves or the wood moves. The marks on your workpiece could look like a repeated chip pattern or a spiral bump. Several of the projects in this book will have chatterwork applied with a chatter tool, where the tool is doing the moving. A few other projects will have a spiral bump pattern, which is the result of the wood doing the moving. The instructions on this page are for creating chatterwork using a chatter tool.

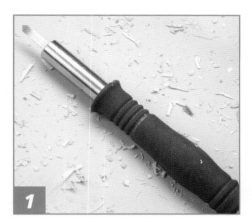

The Stewart Chatter Tool.

On the end of a practice piece of dense wood (with the grain parallel to the lathe), draw a line from the center to the edge. Rotate the line to where a clock hour hand would be at 7:30.

You will be moving the chatter tool along this line, with the blade parallel to the line. This is an end view.

This is the front view. The tool shaft is supported by the tool rest, and nothing should be touching the blade.

This is the view from above. A more closed angle between the face of the tool and the surface of the workpiece will give the tool a better opportunity to chatter.

With a speed of about 2,000 rpm, touch the tip of the tool to the face of the workpiece about ¼" from the center. With light pressure, you should hear chatter. Too much pressure will just cut a groove. Move the tool (along the "7:30 line") adding pressure as the diameter increases. Pressure is increased as the surface speed increases.

If you interrupt the movement of the tool, lift it off, move it over, and set it back down, you can create an un-chattered band for accent.

This is some chatterwork done at about 2,000 rpm. You typically get a finer pattern with a slower speed.

This is a pattern chattered at about 3,000 rpm.

The tip of a skew lying on its side has been used to accentuate the pattern in Photo 9 with some small grooves.

Several examples of patterns and color combinations are shown here.

A chatter pattern can also be applied to the side of a workpiece by holding the tip of the tool low and under the workpiece.

This is a side view. The chatter tool is pressed up against the workpiece.

Some side grain chatter results are shown here.

Another pattern is shown in this photo.

Make some grooves and burn some lines to enhance the pattern.

Finishing

These are the finishing processes I use in my demonstrations and classes. Good cutting techniques will result in a surface on your workpiece that should require only minimal sanding.

The process of sanding involves the use of several grits from coarse to fine. The actual grit numbers will largely depend on your tool techniques. The surface quality of your turnings, right off the tool, will improve as your skills build, providing the opportunity to start with finer grits. A range of grits from about 180 through about 400 would be fine for the projects in this book. Wipe the old sanding grit and dust from your workpiece whenever you switch to a finer grit.

Spray shellac is used as a sealer to even out the appearance of the side and end grain areas of the turnings. Because the shellac in the spray can is "dewaxed," you may apply nearly any finish over it. For teaching and demonstrating, I favor the use of inexpensive Kiwi neutral shoe wax, because it comes in a small, easy-to-open can. Applied with a soft cloth, it works as well as most other waxes. Carnauba wax applied to your workpiece with a buffing wheel adds good protection for handling, in addition to being attractive. Pure carnauba is the hardest of waxes and won't soften from the heat of your hands (causing fingerprints). If you rub the wax directly onto your workpiece, it could cause scratching or bruising on softer surfaces. Buffing can be done after the pieces are off the lathe and anytime a touch-up is needed.

Spray shellac and neutral Kiwi wax (for shoes).

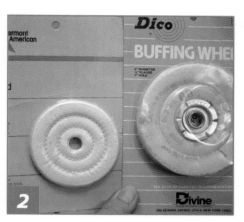

There are many buffing wheels available. I use flannel or muslin wheels that are 4" in diameter.

On the Klein Lathe, an arbor is used to mount the buffing wheel on the spindle. There are many types of arbors available for this use.

It is good to have a wheel dedicated for each different buffing compound used and a separate one just for items finished with black India ink.

Carnauba wax is applied lightly to a spinning buff. Excess wax will cause white streaks in your finish. These can be removed by using a clean buffing wheel. Inset: Pure carnauba wax comes in many forms. Smaller pieces can be remelted and poured into a small mold.

Hang on tightly to your workpiece and press it firmly against the spinning buffing wheel. Rotate your workpiece to polish all surfaces.

Shop Aids

There are many shop aids that make your turning easier and more enjoyable.
Some can be made yourself or can be purchased inexpensively.

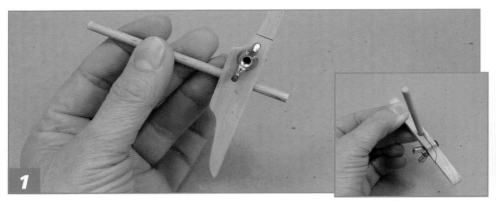

1

If you make boxes or containers, a depth gauge comes in very handy. This was made from a scrap of pine and a ⅛" dowel. Cut a slot and drill a hole for a small bolt and wing nut for adjusting the tension on the dowel. Long wings are great for spanning the opening, and the wooden dowel won't mar your turning.

3

These band saw V blocks consist of a section of 2x4 cut to shape and covered with an anti-slip material used to line drawers. They support a round workpiece as you guide it through the band saw, holding it firmly and keeping your fingers away from the blade.

5

If you cut many glue blocks of a particular size, a plug cutter, used in a drill press, will save a lot of time. This one cuts a 2"-diameter plug. The great thing about this type is that you never have to stop the drill press to extract the pieces. It ejects them as you continue to cut pieces out of ¾"-thick wood.

2

A piece of MDF (medium-density fiberboard) makes a useful sanding disc for the peel-and-stick sandpaper discs. Mount it on a faceplate with double-faced, pressure-sensitive tape for use on the lathe (inset).

4

This is a small sanding drum that may be used on the lathe.

6

The colored pens used in this book are made by Tombow, Staedtler, and Sharpie. The colored ones are chosen because they have a nice paintbrush-type tip with plenty of ink that flows as you apply them to your turnings.

Safety Tips

1 Read and thoroughly understand the label warnings on the lathe and in the owner/operator's manual.

2 Always wear safety goggles or safety glasses. Use side protectors and a full face shield when needed. Because wood dust can be harmful to your respiratory system, use a dust mask or helmet, proper ventilation, and a dust collection system. Wear hearing protection during extended periods of operation.

3 Tie back long hair. Do not wear gloves, loose clothing, jewelry, or any dangling objects that may catch in rotating parts or accessories.

4 Check the owner/operator's manual for proper speed recommendations. Use slower speeds for larger diameter or rough pieces; use increased speed for smaller diameters and pieces that are balanced. If the lathe is shaking or vibrating, lower the speed. If the workpiece vibrates, always stop the machine to check the reason.

5 Make certain that the belt guard or cover is in place. Check that all clamping devices (locks), such as on the tailstock and the toolrest, are tight. Remove chuck keys and adjusting wrenches. Form a habit of checking for these before switching the lathe on.

6 Rotate your workpiece by hand to make sure it clears the toolrest and bed before turning the lathe on. Be sure that the workpiece turns freely and is firmly mounted. It is always safest to turn the lathe off before adjusting the tool rest.

7 Hold turning tools securely on the toolrest in a controlled but comfortable manner. Always use a slower speed when starting, until the workpiece is balanced. Using a slower speed helps to avoid the possibility of an unbalanced piece jumping out of the lathe and striking the operator.

8 Know your capabilities and limits. An experienced woodturner may be capable of techniques and procedures not recommended for beginning turners.

9 When using a faceplate, be certain the workpiece is solidly mounted. When turning between centers, be certain the workpiece is secure.

10 Always remove the toolrest before sanding or polishing operations.

11 Don't overreach; keep proper footing and balance at all times.

12 Keep the lathe in good repair. Check for damaged parts, alignment problems, binding of moving parts, and other conditions that may affect its operation.

13 Keep tools sharp and clean for better and safer performance. Don't force a dull tool. Don't use a tool for a purpose not intended. Keep tools out of reach of children.

14 Consider your work environment. Don't use the lathe in damp or wet locations or in the presence of flammable liquids or gases. Keep your work area well lit.

15 Stay alert. Watch what you are doing, and use common sense. Don't operate a tool when you are tired or under the influence of drugs or alcohol.

16 Guard against electric shock. Inspect electric cords for damage. Avoid the use of extension cords.

17 Never leave the lathe running unattended. Turn the power off, and don't leave the lathe until it comes to a complete stop.

Courtesy *American Woodturner*

Acorn Box

Containers that resemble a shape found in nature, such as an egg, an apple, or a mushroom, have a special appeal. The acorn is a popular shape and makes an attractive box. The cap is a perfect place for some chatterwork. The cap and the nut could be made from contrasting woods.

Finished sizes:
Cap, 1¼" diameter
Nut, 1" diameter

Wood
- For the cap: blank about 1⅜" square by 1¼" long
- For the nut: blank about 1¼" square by 1½" long

Tools and Supplies
- ⅜" gouge
- Round nose scraper
- Square scraper
- Skew
- Parting tool
- Chatter tool
- Felt pens (light and dark brown)
- Cyanocrylate (CA) glue and accelerator
- Sandpaper
- Buffing wheel with carnauba wax
- Shellac and wax

1 Blocks prepared to make two boxes. Blanks for the nuts on the right; blanks for the caps on the left. Arrows indicate grain direction.

2 With the lathe running, use a pencil to make some concentric circles as a target. The target is helpful for centering your workpiece.

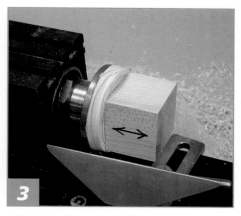

3 Using CA glue, attach the blank for the cap on the target. The grain must be parallel to the lathe bed. (For tips on gluing, see pages 8-9.)

4 Turn down to round using the ⅜" gouge.

5 Adjust the tool rest to support the gouge for the cut across the face.

6 Mark off about ⅞" diameter for the interior of the cap. The outside diameter is about 1¼".

7 Start hollowing with the round nose scraper held flat on the rest.

8 Continue hollowing to a finished depth of about ⅝".

9 Using the left side of the square scraper, cut the inside parallel to the lathe bed, creating a step about ³⁄₁₆" deep.

10 Check with a straightedge to be certain the inside surface is parallel to the bed.

11 Mark the depth of the interior.

12 Shape the rim of the cap with the gouge.

13 Shape most of the top of the cap, leaving a neck about ½" in diameter to support the action of the chatter tool.

14 The skew lying flat on the tool rest can be helpful in refining the shape.

15 Sand the cap. Since this entire surface is to be chattered, it isn't necessary to use more than one grit.

16 Use the chatter tool to create texture on as much of the cap as you can reach. Hold the tool low and under the workpiece to create the side grain chatter. (See chatterwork section, pages 11-12.)

17 Color the cap (light and dark brown were used on this one).

18 Finish just the inside at this time with shellac and wax. The shellac will smear the colors if used on the outside.

19 Finish rough shaping the tip as you cut it away from the glue block.

20 This photo shows the finished interior. Notice the step.

21 Make a target for centering. Then, mount the longer blank onto the glue block with the grain parallel to the lathe bed.

22 True up the sides.

23 True up the face.

24 With a parting tool, cut a short tenon the same diameter as the cap interior.

25 Aim for a fairly snug fit.

26 From the diameter of that tenon, mark a wall thickness of about ⅟₁₆" to establish the diameter of the interior.

27 Hollow most of the interior with the round nose scraper.

28 Straighten the first ¼" of the interior side walls with the square scraper. This will make it easier to do the reverse chucking for turning the tip of the nut.

29 Sandpaper wrapped around a pencil works well for sanding the inside.

30 Use some shellac as a sealer and apply some wax. (See the finishing section on page 13 for more information.)

31 Lengthen the tenon to about ³⁄₁₆", maintaining a tight fit.

32 Press the cap on and do the final shaping for the tip.

33 Use the chatter tool to apply texture.

34 Color the tip to match the rest of the cap.

35 Mark the depth of the interior.

36 Make a parting tool cut, allowing extra wood for shaping the nut.

37 Use the gouge to cut the sides down to the diameter of the tenon.

38 Use a parting tool to reduce the neck area as needed.

39 Check that the wall thickness is uniform.

40 Shape as far as you can with the gouge.

41 Create a tenon on a waste block to fit the interior.

42 Make the tenon about ¼" long with a nice, square shoulder. It should be a snug fit.

43 Press the nut onto the tenon.

44 Finish the tip, taking light cuts with the gouge, holding the piece in place if needed.

45 Sand smooth, carefully adjusting the final fit of the cap with light sanding.

46 Seal and wax the exterior.

47 Buff the nut with carnauba wax.

48 Buff the cap with carnauba wax.

49 The cap should stay on securely, but it should not be too tight.

50 Here is the finished box.

Carrot Pen

Long before the many pen kits were available, woodturners would take the insert out of a Bic ballpoint pen to use inside turned pens of whatever shape they wanted. This project lends itself to lots of creative ideas. A carrot pen would make a nice gift for your favorite gardener, especially if you use green ink, or it could be a cute gift for your favorite Easter Bunny.

This type of pen, well turned in other shapes, done in a pretty wood and nicely finished, makes an attractive desk pen.

Finished size:
6⅜" long

Wood
■ One blank 1" square by 7" long, with a 5/32" hole drilled about 5" deep in one end and band saw cuts for the spur drive in the other end.

Tools and Supplies
■ ⅜" gouge
■ Razor saw and scissors
■ Drill with 5/32"-diameter bit
■ Pliers
■ Bic ballpoint pen (available in green ink, which is perfect for the carrot pens)
■ Orange and green felt pens (Tombow #905, and Staedtler #4 are good oranges)
■ Buffing wheel with carnauba wax

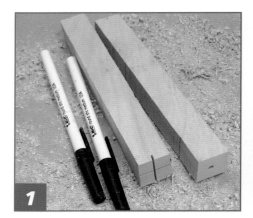

1

When turning small projects using hard wood, to avoid splitting the wood, I suggest making band saw cuts for the spur drive instead of driving the spur in with a mallet. Grain direction is parallel to the lathe.

2

Mount the workpiece with the spur drive engaged in the cuts and the point of the live center inserted into the drilled hole. Use just enough pressure to securely hold the piece. Too much pressure could cause a split.

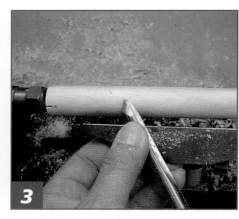

3

Turn down to round using a ⅜" gouge.

4

Mark off a section for the green stem end, leaving enough waste wood at the top for parting off.

5

Shape the top.

6

Shape the carrot's shoulder, and then the body, creating some uneven grooves to simulate the surface of a carrot.

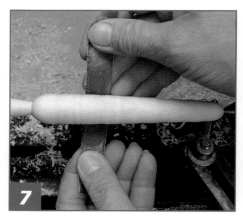

7

Sand smooth.

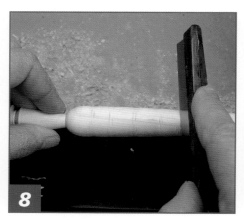

8

With the lathe off, use a razor saw to make quite a few short, random cuts across the carrot body.

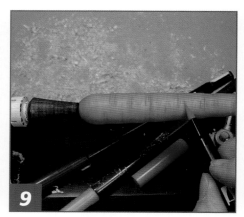

9

Color the carrot with pens, inks, or paints, making certain to get color into all of the cuts.

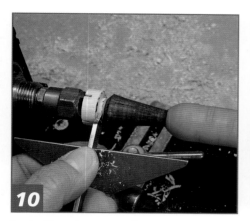

10 Part off at the top end.

11 Sand and color the top.

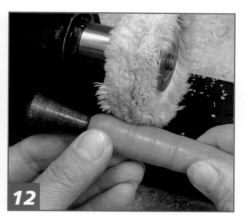

12 Buff with carnauba wax on the buffing wheel.

13 With pliers, carefully remove an insert from a Bic ballpoint pen.

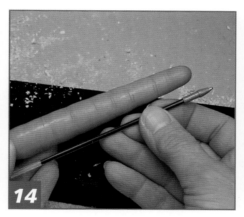

14 Measure the drilled hole for depth, shorten the insert with scissors if needed, and push the insert into place.

15 Start making your list!

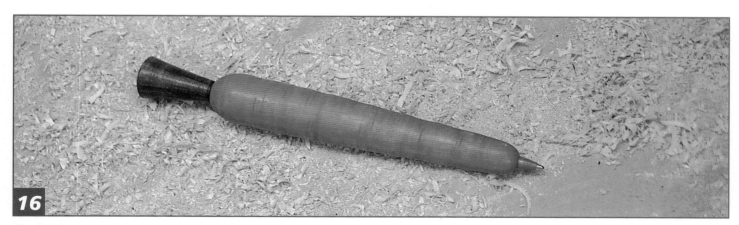

16 The finished pen.

Sunburst Earrings

The desire for light, comfortable, attractive earrings that didn't look like little turned chair legs hanging on my ears led to this idea. They are comfortable to wear and are an ideal project for a pretty piece of wood. If you are using wood with strong grain lines, the earrings can appear to be smiling (or even frowning) if you pay attention to the orientation of the lines. Turning end grain thin with chatterwork is the challenge of this project.

Finished size:
2" long

Wood
- One blank about 2¼" diameter by 1" long (should make two pairs)

Tools and Supplies
- ⅜" gouge
- Round nose scraper
- Parting tool
- Skew
- Chatter tool
- Razor saw
- Rotary tool or drill with ³⁄₆₄"-diameter bit
- Colored pens (Tombow #055–yellow)
- Black India ink (faux ebony pair)
- 18g jump rings ⁷⁄₁₆" diameter
- Ear wires
- Buffing wheel with carnauba wax

1 Preparation: Mount the block with the grain direction parallel to the lathe bed.

2 Turn down to round using your ⅜" gouge.

3 The round nose scraper has been sharpened on the end and along the side.

4 Create a shallow, concave recess about ¼" deep with the round nose scraper.

5 Sand it smooth. Since this entire surface is to be chattered, it isn't necessary to use more than one grit.

6 Use the chatter tool to create a pattern across the surface. To prevent the grain from splitting out, stop before you get to the edge.

7 Color the pattern a sunny yellow.

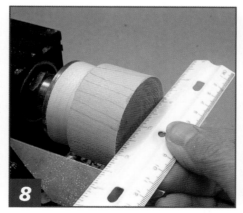

8 Use a straightedge to visually check the depth.

9 Make a parting tool cut down to about a ¾" diameter, adding about 1/16" in depth for the thickness of the earrings.

10 Carefully shape the back side as far as you can reach. A good thickness to aim for is ⅟₁₆".

11 Sand the back side and edges smooth. (See the finishing section on page 13.)

12 Use the parting tool to roughly shape the rest of the back.

13 Part it off completely.

14 On a waste block, create a convex curve to roughly match the concave curve of your workpiece.

15 Check to see that it doesn't rock on any high spots.

16 Apply some double-faced tape to the waste block.

17 Carefully center the workpiece on the waste block.

18 A bit of pressure will hold it in place long enough to finish the back side.

19 With light cuts, refine the back side using the ³⁄₈" gouge. You will only need to be working on the center area.

20 Using the skew on its side will smooth out any remaining ridges.

21 Sand the back side.

22 Apply color to match the front.

23 Carefully remove your workpiece.

24 Remove the tape, and then use your waste block to support the earring blank while sawing.

25 Cut it in half with a small razor saw.

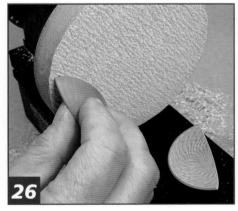

26 With 220-grit sandpaper on a sanding disc, create a convex curve on each piece.

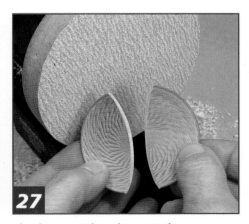

27 Check to see that they match.

28 Sand matching curves along the upper outside edges.

29 Check to see that the curves match.

30 Drill a small hole for the jump ring in the upper corner. (The jump ring is used to connect the earring to the ear wire.)

31 Hand sand the edges smooth and apply color.

32 Buff with carnauba wax.

33 Hold them securely, with plenty of support, while buffing.

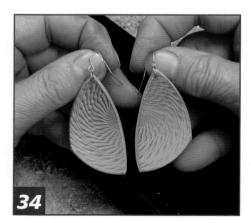

34 Attach the ear wires to the earrings with jump rings.

As an alternative, you could make a faux ebony pair. To do this, proceed as you would to make the yellow pair up to Step 5. Then, follow the steps below.

1 Apply black India ink with a Q-tip over the surface before and after you chatter.

2 Color the edge and turn the back side.

3 Sand.

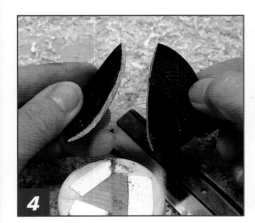

4 Cut in half, the thickness should be about 1/16".

5 By holding the earring blanks in a different way, you can create crescent-shaped earrings.

6 Color the edges, drill holes, and buff with carnauba wax.

Spiral Chatter Eggs

In woodturning, a chatter pattern can be the result of either tool movement (see the chatter tool page 11) or wood movement. I chose this project to demonstrate a type of chatter pattern that happens when the wood moves. The unique pattern has the appearance of smooth spiral bumps and often shows up when turning thin spindles or cutting across the bottom of a thin bowl. This exercise demonstrates the consequence of bevel pressure during the cutting process. Since the wood movement (resulting in the spiral pattern) is often caused by excess bevel pressure, I like to call this an "exercise in tool control." To remove or prevent the pattern, the opposite action is necessary. You must make the cut without bevel pressure, just bevel contact. Once you understand this process, you will find interesting places to use the pattern, and you will also understand how to eliminate it. The egg shapes were chosen because they are easy shapes for experimentation and can be added to your Easter basket.

Finished sizes:
2¼" high, 1¾"-diameter

Wood
- One blank about 2" in diameter by 2¾" long

Tools and Supplies
- ⅜" gouge
- Parting tool
- Skew
- Colored pens (in pastel colors of choice)
- Sandpaper
- Buffing wheel with carnauba wax

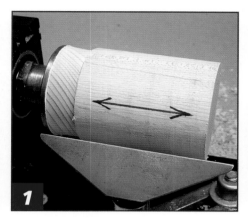

1 Mount the workpiece on a glue block with the grain parallel to the lathe.

2 Turn it round using the ⅜" gouge.

3 About ¼" to the right of the glue line, make a parting tool cut.

4 Make the cut about ¼" wide down to about 1" in diameter for a neck.

5 Start shaping the egg using the ⅜" gouge.

6 Complete the egg shape.

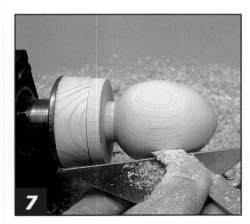

7 A skew lying on its side is useful for lightly refining the shape.

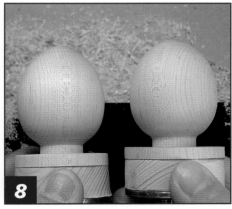

8 For this project, two eggs are being used as examples.

9 Reduce the neck to about ½" or ⅝" diameter. Experiment with different diameters.

To make the spiral pattern, apply heavy pressure with the bevel while taking a light cut. Shavings should be coming off the tool just below the tip. This egg was turning at about 2,000 rpm.

The idea is to push against the wood, causing it to move. You will definitely hear it bumping. This egg was turning at about 3,000 rpm.

This is the result so far. If you don't care for your results, repeat the cut with bevel contact, but no bevel pressure, to remove the pattern.

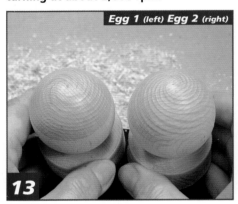

You can pick up where you left off and finish the cuts.

Lay the bevel of the gouge against the surface, apply pressure, and cut toward the headstock.

Finish the cut as far as you can reach.

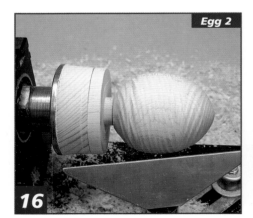

This photograph shows a cut made across the middle toward the headstock.

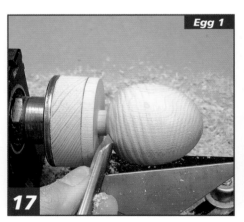

This is the other egg after being cut at 2,000 rpm.

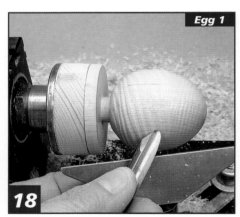

Making another pass across the center toward the tailstock on this one.

19 These examples are the result of different speeds and different neck diameters. The surfaces are right off the tool without any sanding.

Egg 1 (left) Egg 2 (right)

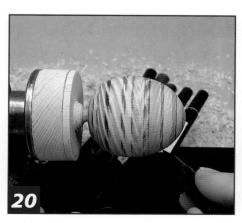

20 Apply the pastel colors of your choice.

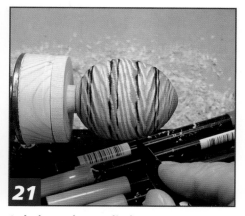

21 A darker color applied as an accent seems to make all of the other colors brighter.

22 Part off at the neck, maintaining the egg shape.

23 Hand sand the end smooth.

24 Buffing with carnauba wax will help to protect the colors.

25 Finished eggs. Do plenty of experimenting. If you aren't pleased with your results and want to remove the spiral pattern, support the workpiece with your fingers, to prevent wood movement, as you make a light cut with the gouge. It is important to realize that a sharp tool will require less pressure. Remember to keep the bevel in contact with the wood, but without any bevel pressure.

Letter Opener

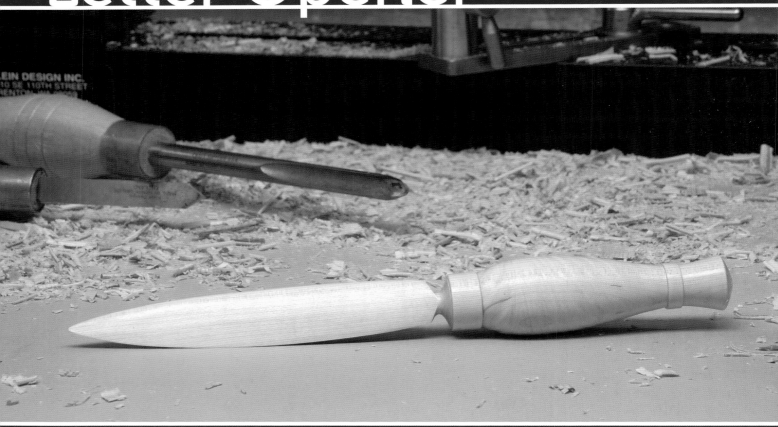

My good friend, Wally Dickerman, taught me how to make letter openers. As a challenge, I have added a spiral chatter pattern to the handle. The process of creating the pattern on the handle and the shaping of the blade make this project unique. For additional information about the spiral pattern, see the Spiral Chatter Eggs demonstration on page 32. A letter opener is a good project to show off an attractive piece of wood.

Finished size:
8⅜" long

Wood
- One blank about 1" square by 9" long with band saw cuts for the spur drive

Tools and Supplies
- ⅜" gouge
- Parting tool
- Skew
- Belt or disc sander
- Band saw
- 3M pad
- Buffing wheel with carnauba wax
- Shellac and wax

1 The grain direction needs to be parallel to the lathe bed. The band saw cuts eliminate having to pound the spur in with a mallet.

2 Mount the workpiece between centers with the spur drive engaging the band saw cuts.

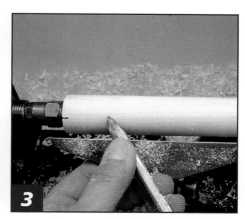

3 Turn down to round using a ⅜" gouge.

4 Mark off a section about 4" long for the handle.

5 With the parting tool, make ¼"-deep cuts above the spur and at the 4" mark.

6 Shape the blade with a skew or with the gouge.

7 The blade should have a nice taper.

8 Use the gouge to shape the handle.

9 Turn a narrow neck between the handle and the blade and make a fairly deep parting tool cut at the spur drive end.

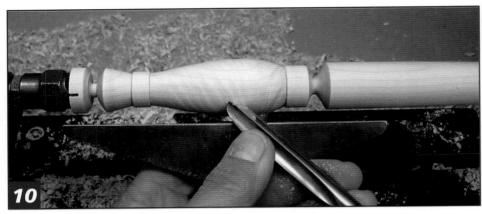

10

This will create the opportunity for a spiral pattern to happen when a light cut is taken using extra bevel pressure against the wood (same technique as the spiral eggs on pages 32-35). The wood will flex. Make a pass going downhill in each direction from the largest diameter.

11

It's likely that you will only need to sand the areas without the spiral pattern. Sand the neck area. You don't need to sand the blade at this time.

12

Apply sealer and wax.

13

A 3M pad with wax helps burnish the spirals.

14

Part off at the handle end.

15

Hand sand the parting cut smooth.

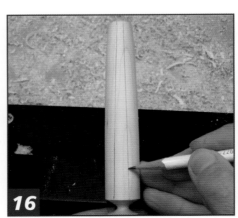

16

To shape the blade, first mark off the thickness from neck to tip.

17

Cut away the excess with the band saw.

Draw the silhouette of the blade.

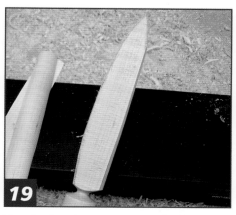

Use the band saw to cut to the line.

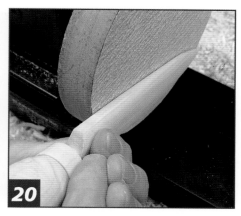

You can use a belt or disc sander to shape the blade.

Use a coarse grit, about 100 grit, for quick wood removal and rough shaping.

Check the silhouette for symmetry.

Check the thickness of the blade for symmetry as you remove wood.

Change to a finer grit, about 220 grit, to refine the shape.

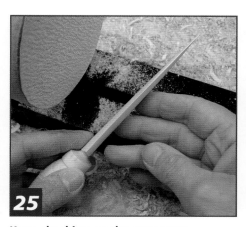

Keep checking on the symmetry.

Hand sand with the grain before progressing to a finer grit.

27 Shape the tip carefully. Don't make it too thin.

28 Roll the back side of the blade against the disc sander.

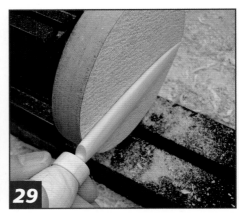

29 The blade should be well shaped and durable, but not too thin.

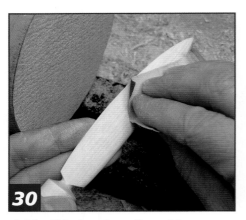

30 Finish off by hand sanding with the grain.

31 Check the tip for durability.

32 Check the thickness. If it is too thick, it won't function well; if it is too thin, it will break easily.

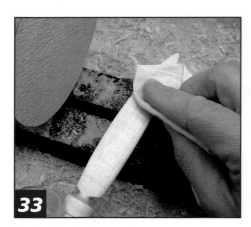

33 Seal with shellac and wax.

34 Buff with carnauba wax on the buffing wheel.

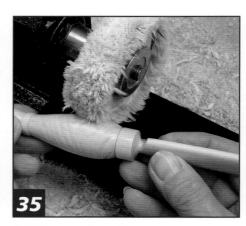

35 Buff the spirals well.

36

The spiral pattern on the handle adds an
interesting texture.

37

Finished letter opener.

Stir Fry Spatula

Wooden kitchen utensils have been used for centuries. Many of us remember our grandmother's wooden cooking spoons and the beautiful patina that developed from years of use. In my kitchen, a spatula like this is kept near the stove, used almost daily, and even put through the dishwasher. This project combines a slightly unusual process of turning a spatula profile combined with a spindle turned handle. Final shaping with a band saw and sander creates a functional item for yourself or for your favorite cook to enjoy. These techniques could be used to make a variety of kitchen utensils.

Finished size:
9¼" long

Wood
- ☐ One blank ¾" thick by 2" wide by 10" long

Tools and Supplies
- ☐ ⅜" gouge
- ☐ Skew
- ☐ Band saw
- ☐ Wire for burning lines
- ☐ Mineral oil

1 Draw the basic silhouette.

2 Band saw to the general shape, cutting the handle to ¾" square with band saw cuts for the spur drive.

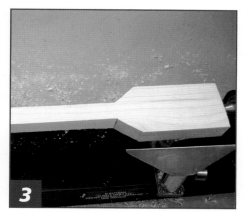

3 Mount the blank between centers with the spatula end centered on the live center point. Keep the speed below 1,800 rpm to start.

4 Using the ⅜" gouge, start by shaping the spatula end. Turn that area down to the desired shape.

5 Blend the shape toward the handle using the ⅜" gouge.

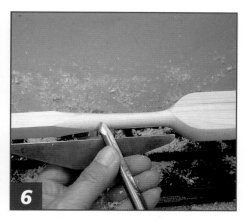

6 Remove the corners and shape the handle as you progress toward the headstock.

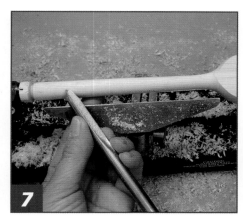

7 You could speed up the lathe a bit as you turn the handle down to the desired diameter.

8 When you are turning long, thin spindles, you may get a spiral pattern. This is caused by wood movement as a result of excess tool pressure or possibly of worn or poor quality bearings in the live center. If you like the pattern, you could keep it. See the Spiral Chatter Eggs section on page 32 for more information.

9 To prevent wood movement, you could support the workpiece in an overhand grip like this.

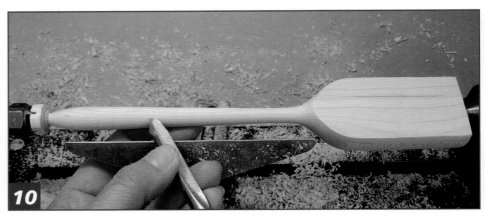

10 Another way to prevent wood movement is to reach under the workpiece to support it from below. Your tool must have bevel contact, but no bevel pressure pushing against the wood, causing it to move.

11 Sand the handle. You don't need to sand the spatula part at this time.

12 Cut a few grooves with the point of the skew and burn some lines for decoration. (See the burned line section on page 10.)

13 Turn down the end of the handle to about ⅛" or smaller and sand that area.

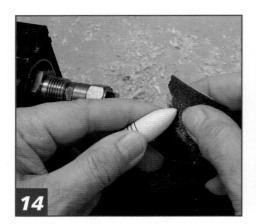

14 Part the spatula off and sand the end by hand.

15 On the side of the spatula, draw some curved cutting lines for the shape you want.

16 With a band saw, the excess can be easily removed by carefully holding the spatula on its side as you cut.

17 Now you can customize your spatula for either left- or right-handed cooks.

18 Refine the shape using a drum sander on the lathe or the belt sander in your shop. For quick shaping, start with about 100-grit.

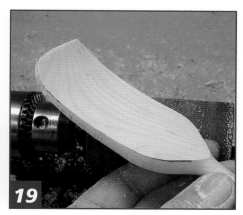

19 When you achieve the thickness and shape you want, you can then refine all of the surfaces with a finer grit, such as 220.

20 Hand sanding will probably be necessary for a good, functional surface.

21 For durability, be sure to make all of the edges smooth, but not too thin.

22 Soaking wooden cooking utensils overnight in mineral oil, and then wiping them dry provides a good, serviceable finish. Reapply the finish as desired.

23 Finished spatula. Our grandmothers probably weren't concerned about applying a finish to their cooking spoons. They were just washed and put away.

Spin Top

Evidence of spin tops can be found in nearly every culture throughout history. They appeal to all ages and, as a woodturning project, provide a great skill-building exercise. The spin top provides an opportunity to practice chatterwork and then to brighten it up with color. These are some of the reasons I like to turn tops in workshops and demonstrations. This is a true Bonnie Klein "classic" and the perfect project to introduce new or young turners to the lathe.

Finished size:
1⅞"-diameter

Wood
- One blank about 2" diameter by 2½" long

Tools and Supplies
- ⅜" gouge
- Skew
- Parting tool
- Chatter tool
- Felt pens (colors of choice)
- Buffing wheel with carnauba wax

1. Mount the workpiece onto the glue block and true it up using a ⅜" gouge.

2. Adjust the tool rest at an angle to provide support for the tool all the way through the cut. Start with angle cuts across the corner.

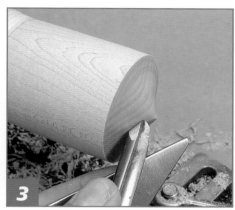

3. Shavings should be coming off the tool just below the tip with the bevel rubbing.

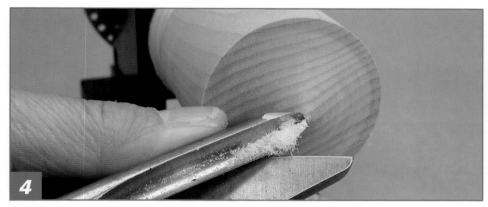

4. The height of the toolrest should allow the point of the tool to arrive exactly level with the center of the top, without having to reach up or down.

5. Sand the area and apply a light base color, holding the pen pointed down to avoid damage to the pen tip.

6. Apply a chatter pattern (see the chatter directions on pages 11-12) to the bottom of the spin top, stopping before you reach the edge to avoid tearing out the grain.

7. With the lathe on, carefully add some darker colors to just the tops of the bumps of the chatter pattern. Silver adds a nice sparkle.

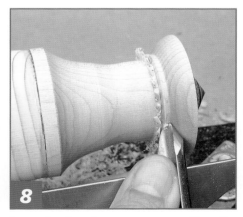

8. Start shaping the upper part and handle, stopping about ¼" above the glue joint to maintain support.

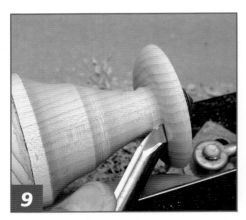

Turn the handle to a diameter of about ⅝", and shape and sand the top surface.

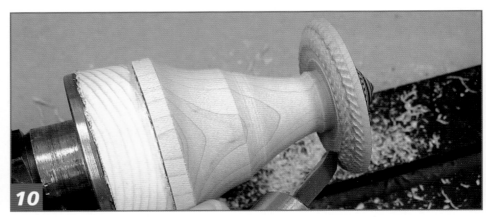

The larger diameter will give support for the pressure of the chatter tool. Apply the base color before chattering. The chatter tool moves along a line that would be similar to the hour hand on a clock at 4:30.

Finish all of the chatterwork and coloring before you start to shape the handle.

When the handle gets thin, use your finger for support and position the bevel of the tool against the wood as you make light cuts.

Sand the handle area and apply color stripes if desired.

You can use a gouge, with the bevel rubbing, to part off the top, creating a pointed end.

You could also use a skew chisel to make V-cuts, creating a pointed end.

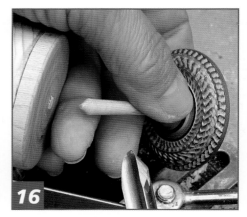

A point on the handle will allow you to spin the top upside down as well as right side up.

Sand the tip of the handle if necessary.

Apply carnauba wax to the buffing wheel.

Buff the top.

Buff all sides.

The carnauba wax will protect the colors and keep them fresh-looking.

Finished spin top.

Group of tops. Spin tops are fun to make and fun for all ages to play with. Make a few with chatterwork and bright colors and see for yourself.

Experiment with different colors and ideas. This is a jack-o-lantern spin top I turned and colored for Halloween.

Tool Handle

If you use or make tools, you might have need for a custom-fit handle. This project utilizes a plumbing compression nut as a ferrule and provides the experience of turning brass with your regular high-speed steel (HSS) tools. The tool handle is great for skill building and is a great place to experiment with new techniques, shapes, and sizes. You will enjoy using a tool with a handle that fits your hand.

Finished size:
4" long

Wood
- One blank 1" square by 4½" long

Tools and Supplies
- ⅜" gouge
- Parting tool
- Chatter tool
- Pliers or wrench
- Drill with ⅛"-diameter bit
- Jacobs chuck
- Wire for burning lines
- Brass compression nut for the ferrule (from the plumbing department)
- Colored felt pens (colors of choice)
- Shellac and wax
- Buffing wheel with carnauba wax

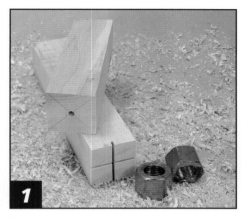

1 Make band saw cuts for the spur drive on one end and drill a ⅛" pilot hole in the other end. This will ensure that your tool will be centered in the finished handle.

2 The grain direction needs to be parallel to the lathe bed. Mount the workpiece between centers.

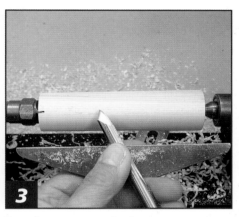

3 Turn down to round using your ⅜" gouge.

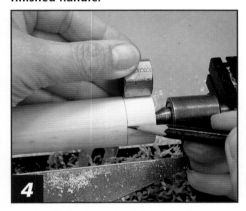

4 Mark off the length of the ferrule.

5 With a parting tool, turn a short tenon that will extend through the smaller hole in the compression nut.

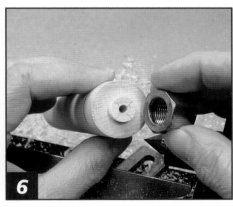

6 Check the diameter of the short tenon to be sure it fits through the smaller hole.

7 Turn down another section for the interior of the ferrule.

8 Check the length. The wood should be even with the outside end of the ferrule.

9 The diameter should be large enough to require pliers or a wrench to screw it on.

10 The ferrule should sit all the way down against the square shoulder.

11 Mount the workpiece between centers with the ferrule in place.

12 Turn down the brass, taking light cuts with your ⅜" gouge.

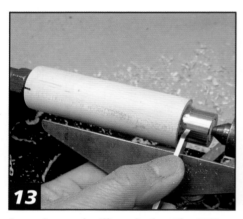

13 A parting tool will work also. The HSS tools will cut because they are much harder than the brass.

14 Sand the ferrule and polish it with a metal polish if desired. 220-grit sandpaper could be used to achieve a nice satin finish.

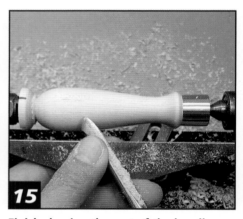

15 Finish shaping the rest of the handle.

16 Add some interesting texture with the chatter tool. (See the side chatter tips on pages 11-12.)

17 Burned lines will accent the chatter texture.

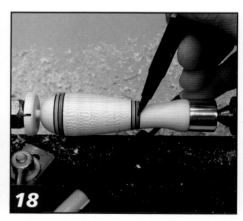

18 Colors will enhance your handles and could be used to more easily distinguish one tool from another.

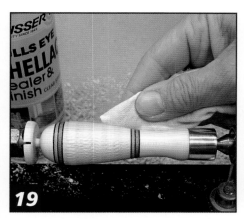

19 Seal the surface with spray shellac. Be careful not to smear the colors.

20 Part off at the headstock end.

21 Hand sand the parted end to make it smooth.

22 Buff with carnauba wax.

23 Drill the hole for the tool by holding the handle parallel to the lathe bed and pushing it onto a spinning drill bit driven by the headstock, or use a drill press. If you know ahead of time what tool you are making the handle for, you could predrill the correct size hole instead of the ⅛" pilot hole.

24 Finished tool handle.

Whistle

When I was about ten years old, I remember reading instructions for making a willow whistle in an issue of *Boy's Life* magazine. In later years, as a turner looking for projects to make, I recalled the basics of the instruction. This project has developed through trial and error. When I do this as a demonstration, I like to say it is the perfect gift for grandpas to give to their grandchildren—as the kids are leaving to go home.

The techniques involve drilling a hole on the lathe and burning lines.

Finished size:
4" long

Wood
- One blank about 1" square by 4½" long with a ⅜" hole drilled about 3" deep
- One ½" diameter dowel

Tools and Supplies
- ⅜" gouge
- Parting tool
- Chatter tool
- Drill with ⅜"-diameter bit
- Jacobs chuck
- Disc sander with 220-grit disc
- Depth gauge
- Razor saw
- Felt pens (colors of choice)
- Wire for burning lines
- Screw eye
- Buffing wheel with carnauba wax

1

Predrilled whistle blanks and ½" dowels.

2

If you would like to drill the hole on the lathe, locate the center for the tailstock end.

3

Make a starter hole with a hand drill to help center the drill bit, which is held in a Jacobs chuck on the headstock.

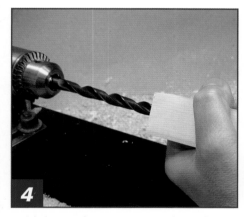

4

Hold the workpiece against the tailstock and aligned with the drill bit.

5

Holding the workpiece securely, use the tailstock to push it onto the drill bit with the lathe running. Clear the chips as necessary to allow efficient cutting.

6

To make a plug for driving the workpiece, use a Jacobs chuck to hold a section of ½" dowel with about 1" protruding. Turn a tenon about ⅝" long with a square shoulder as a stop.

7

The tenon should fit the ⅜" hole very tightly, as this will drive the workpiece. If you find that it slips, try moistening the tenon.

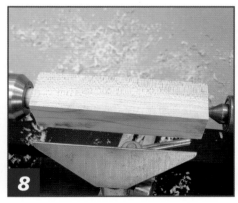

8

Mount the workpiece between centers, seated all the way onto the tenon, and turn it round using the ⅜" gouge.

9

Mark off a section ⅝" long for the mouthpiece and another section ½" long for the notch area.

small woodturning projects **with** Bonnie Klein |

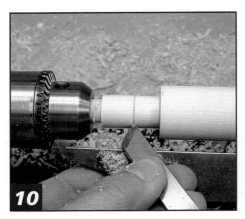

10 Turn this area down to about a ⅝" diameter. Make a groove ⅝" from the end with the point of a skew to reestablish the top of the notch.

11 Burn a decorative line in the groove with a wire.

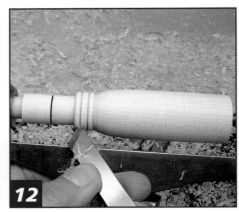

12 Shape the rest of the whistle. The skew is useful in making shallow V-shaped cuts.

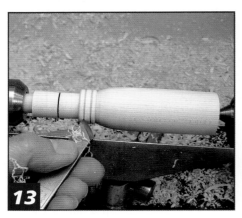

13 Flip it over to cut the other side of the V. For this, the skew is lying flat on the rest.

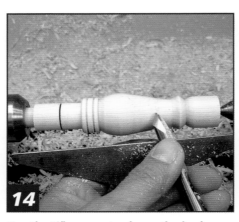

14 Use the ⅜" gouge to shape the body.

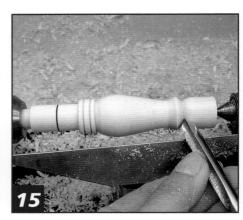

15 Keep the bevel rubbing while cutting the shapes.

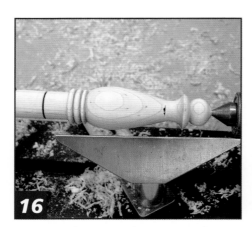

16 Oops! Don't cut too deep. Remember, there is a hole down the center. This small hole was easy to patch with a bit of wood filler.

17 You can check the depth with a pencil before starting.

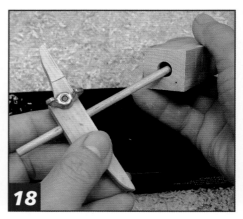

18 You can also check it with the depth gauge.

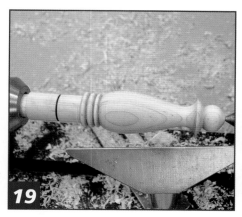

19 Sand the whistle.

20 Add some side grain chatter texture. (See page 12 for more information on side grain chatter.)

21 Burn some accent lines and add colors of choice.

22 Using a razor saw, cut a notch not quite halfway through.

23 The top of the notch is perpendicular to the whistle.

24 Using the parting tool, make one cut on the tenon to use as a grip and another cut for parting off.

25 The tenon needs to be long enough to reach the top of the notch.

26 Sand it down a little, so it isn't so tight, and then part the tenon completely off.

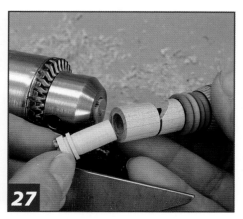

27 You should be able to slide the tenon easily in and out of your whistle as you adjust for the best and loudest sound.

28 Sand a flat on the tenon and slide it into place with the flat up. Blow the whistle to test it.

29 You might need to make the notch bigger or the flat larger. This is where trial and error comes into play.

30 The flat should be level and even with the top of the notch.

31 When you get a good sound, use one tiny drop of glue on the back side of the plug to hold it in place.

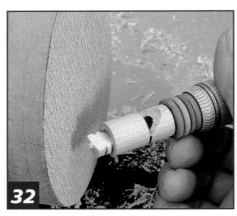

32 This is what remains of the plug.

33 Sand off the part of the plug that protrudes beyond the end of the whistle.

34 Sand a bevel on the underside of the mouthpiece and hand sand all of the edges smooth.

35 This creates a nicely shaped mouthpiece.

36 Buff the finished whistle with carnauba wax and add a tiny screw eye for a string if desired.

Yo-Yo

There are many toys suitable for making on the lathe. This is a project that will relate to all ages. I have developed the techniques for this project to make it fairly simple for young turners. A jig for holding the workpieces is made using a faceplate with a waste block and a length of dowel. Because chatterwork will be used for decoration, the blanks must be end grain.

This has been a successful and popular project with Scouting and 4-H groups. A yo-yo can be made in many sizes, and a smaller diameter will fit a smaller hand or a smaller pocket. Try turning them in other sizes. If you have some wood with interesting grain, you certainly could make your yo-yos side grain (grain direction would be perpendicular to the lathe axis). You just won't be able to decorate with chatterwork.

Finished sizes:
2½"-diameter, 1¼" wide

Wood
- ■ Two end-grain blanks for each yo-yo ¾" thick by 2½" diameter
- ■ ⁵⁄₁₆" and ½" diameter hard maple dowels (short pieces)

Tools and Supplies
- ■ ⅜" gouge
- ■ Skew
- ■ Chatter tool
- ■ Drill with ½"- and ⁵⁄₁₆"-diameter bits
- ■ Jacobs chuck
- ■ Faceplate with waste block for jig
- ■ Dividers and profile gauge
- ■ Felt pens (colors of choice)
- ■ Commercial yo-yo strings
- ■ Shellac and wax
- ■ Buffing wheel with carnauba wax

1 To prepare the end-grain blanks, locate the center of each half. Arrows show grain direction.

2 Drill ⁵⁄₁₆"-diameter holes about ⅜" deep for the axle. The axle is about ¾" long. These holes must be perpendicular to the faces. Sand the faces smooth to avoid snagging the yo-yo string.

3 To prepare the mounting block or jig, face it off flat, locate the center, and create a small recess for the drill bit to center on.

4 Use a ½" drill bit held in a Jacobs chuck in the tailstock.

5 Drill a hole about ⅜" deep.

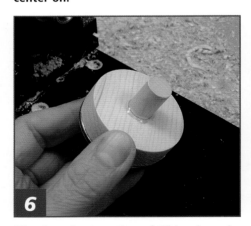

6 Glue in a short section of ½" hard maple dowel. This will last for many yo-yos.

7 Turn down the dowel for a tight press fit in a ⁵⁄₁₆" hole.

8 Check the face of the mounting block to be certain it is absolutely flat.

9 The length of the dowel needs to be a bit shorter than the ⅜"-deep hole in the yo-yo blank.

10 Press on one of the yo-yo halves, until it rests all the way down onto the flat surface of the mounting block without any gap.

11 Alternately, turn down the sides of both halves.

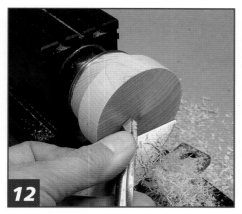

12 True up the outside faces of both halves.

13 It is a good idea to make a reference mark on the jig and on each of the pieces, so they can be relocated on the jig exactly the same each time.

14 Check to see that the halves are the same thickness.

15 Check to see that the diameters are the same.

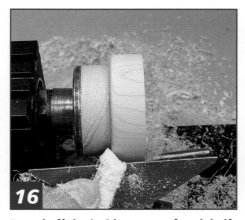

16 Round off the inside corner of each half.

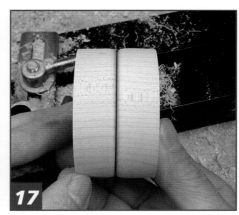

17 Check to see that they match.

18 Draw a reference line on the circumference of each half an equal distance from the face.

19 Start shaping each half. Use the line to help shape each half identically.

20 A skew lying on its side helps to refine the shapes.

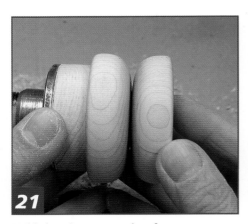

21 Hold the pieces together for comparison.

22 A profile gauge might be of help.

23 Use dividers to mark identical lines on each piece.

24 These lines are boundaries for the chatterwork.

25 Use the tip of the skew to create small V-cuts to enhance the boundary lines.

26 Flip the skew over to cut the other side of the V.

27 Use the chatter tool to create a pattern between the lines. (See the section on chatterwork, pages 11-12, for more information.)

28 It isn't possible to create identical patterns, but they should be close enough.

29 A little extra attention to the detailing of the V-shaped grooves will achieve more identical pieces.

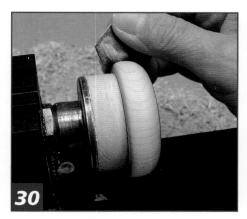

30 Sand the pieces.

31 Add some colors of choice. Light and dark brown were used here.

32 Use shellac as a sealer, being careful not to smear the colors, and then wax.

33 Buff the yo-yo halves with carnauba wax.

34 For the axle, use a piece of ⁵⁄₁₆" dowel ¾" long. Use some spacers ¹⁄₁₆" thick, made from scrap wood, and dry fit the yo-yo before gluing it.

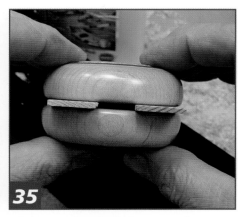

35 When you glue the halves together, the spacers will ensure an even gap all around. Line up the grain before gluing. Add a string to your finished yo-yo.

Honey (Bee) Dipper

This is an easy project featuring the additional shaping of a honey bee body on the handle. As a kitchen utensil, this would be an ideal gift for kids to turn for mom or grandmother. Variations in size and type of wood offer opportunities for interesting designs.

Finished size:
6½" long

Wood
- One blank, about 1" square by 7" long with band saw cuts for the spur drive

Tools and Supplies
- ⅜" gouge
- Parting tool
- Yellow and black felt pens, ink, or paint
- Buffing wheel with carnauba wax

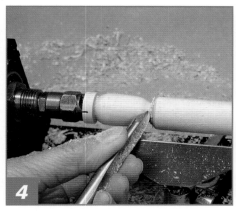

1 Three blanks prepared with band saw cuts for the spur drive.

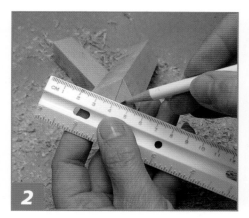

2 Locate the center of the blank for the live center point, using a ruler held across the corners.

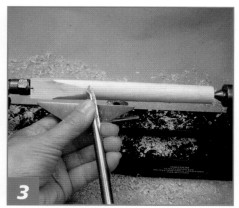

3 Mount between centers and turn the workpiece down to round using a ⅜" gouge.

4 Use the ⅜" gouge to shape the dipper part, but to maintain support, don't make the neck or the waste wood near the spur too narrow at this time.

5 With a parting tool, cut several slots, evenly spaced, down to about ⁵⁄₁₆" in diameter. A thinner parting tool may make more attractive slots.

6 Sand the slots smooth.

7 Finish shaping the handle before turning a couple of beads for the honey bee's body. Leave a little waste wood for sawing off. Use your finger for support to prevent wood movement.

8 Sand the end of the dipper after reducing it to the desired diameter.

9 Sand the handle after all of the shaping has been done.

10 Apply the black color to the bee body. Burned lines help to prevent colors from running.

11 When you apply the yellow color, don't get the pen near the black ink.

12 Cut off both ends with a razor saw. Do this with the lathe turned off.

13 Hand sand the dipper end and the stinger end.

14 Put a black dot on the end of the handle for the stinger.

15 You can soak the dipper in mineral oil and wipe it dry as a finish, or you could buff it with carnauba wax on the buffing wheel.

16 Finished honey (bee) dipper.

Purse Mirror

This project is perfect for a quick and useful gift and is a great way to show off some spectacular chatterwork. Because chatterwork will be used for decoration, the blanks must be end grain. The techniques for this project involve reverse chucking and cutting a recess.

Finished size:
2¾"-diameter

Wood
- One end-grain blank ½" thick by 3" in diameter
- 2" diameter beveled mirror

Tools and Supplies
- ⅜" gouge
- Square scraper
- Parting tool
- Dividers
- Double-faced tape
- CA (cyanoacrylate) glue and accelerator
- Paper for burning lines
- Shellac and wax
- Buffing wheel with carnauba wax

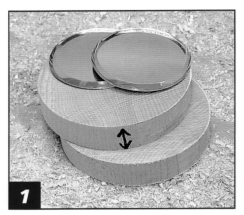

1 Mirrors and ½" end-grain blanks for two purse mirrors.

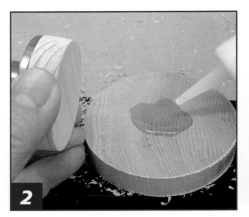

2 Mount the workpiece onto the glue block using CA glue on one side and accelerator on the other side.

3 Center the faceplate with the glue block onto the workpiece.

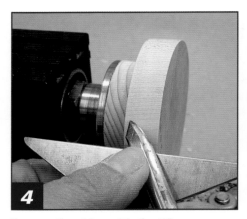

4 True up the sides with the ⅜" gouge.

5 Adjust the tool rest to provide support for the tool as the cut is made across the face.

6 Set a pair of dividers to the diameter of the mirror.

7 Transfer that measurement to the workpiece. With the lathe running and the left side resting on the tool rest, touch the wood with only the left point to create a line at the desired diameter when it appears under the right point of the dividers.

8 Start removing wood with the gouge (bevel rubbing), leaving a small stump in the center to serve as a temporary depth gauge. The recess needs to be about ¼" deep.

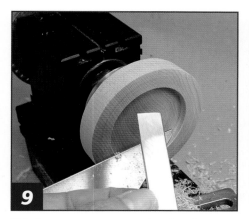

This is a square scraper that has been sharpened on the end and on the left side.

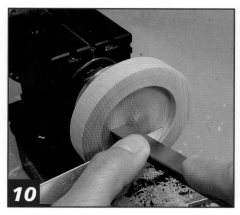

Finish creating the recess, using the square scraper.

Check to see that the depth is ¼", that the side of the recess is exactly parallel to the lathe bed, and that the bottom is flat.

Be sure the mirror fits.

Shape the edge and apply chatter.

You can use the point of a skew to cut small grooves to frame the chatter pattern.

The edge of a small piece of paper held in the grooves with the lathe running at a fast speed will create nice, decorative burn marks. (For more information on this technique, see page 10.)

After sanding, apply some spray shellac as a sealer, making sure it penetrates the end grain chatterwork thoroughly, and then apply wax.

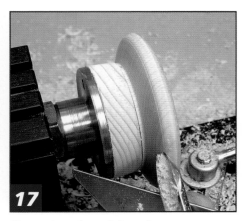

Shape the edge of the mirror.

18 Shape the back side of the mirror as far as you can reach.

19 Part off the workpiece by cutting through the glue block.

20 If you part right at the glue line, there won't be much clean-up needed.

21 Use a wood such as pine as a waste block for reverse chucking the project. The wood you choose for your waste block should be softer than the wood of your project to avoid damage to your project. Using a parting tool, create a tenon almost ¼" long with a good square shoulder for the workpiece to bottom out on.

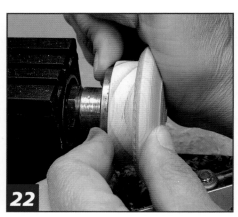

22 It should fit tightly and run true.

23 Shape the back, with the tool rest oriented across the workpiece for tool support.

24 Apply a chatter pattern where desired. If you speed up the lathe to about 3,000 rpm and apply more pressure with the chatter tool, you should get an attractive, heavy pattern.

25 Create some grooves with the tip of the skew (held flat on the tool rest) and burn some more lines to set off the pattern.

26 This is a view of the pattern before finishing.

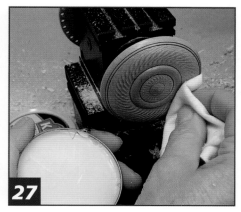

27 Apply the shellac as a sealer, followed by some wax.

28 Double-faced tape works well to hold the mirror in place and can be removed if necessary. Heat from a lamp will relax the tape fibers if you need to replace the mirror.

29 Finished front view.

30 Finished back view.

Resources

KLEIN DESIGN, INC.
425-226-5937
www.bonnieklein.com

**AMERICAN ASSOCIATION
OF WOODTURNERS**
651-484-9094
www.woodturner.org
Quarterly publication
Membership directory
Local chapters
Instructional videos

THE WOODTURNING CENTER
215-923-8000
www.woodturningcenter.org
Books, archives, and exhibitions
Quarterly publication

Miscellaneous Supplies

Brass ferrules	Hardware store plumbing department
Shellac	Hardware stores or large home center stores
Kiwi Boot Polish	Most supermarkets and drug stores
Sharpie Pens	Office supply stores
Stainless wire	Sporting goods stores as fishing leader
Colored pens	Art supply stores or arts and crafts stores
India Ink	Office supply or art stores
Razor saw	Hobby shops or home center stores
Yo-yo strings	Toy stores or sporting good stores
Hardwood dowels	Wood dealers or lumber yards

Look for These Books at Your Local Bookstore or Specialty Retailer or at *www.FoxChapelPublishing.com*

**Christmas Ornaments for
Woodworking, Revised Edition**
ISBN 978-1-56523-788-9 **$16.99**

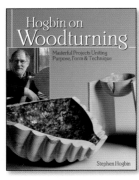

Hogbin on Woodturning
ISBN 978-1-56523-752-0 **$24.99**

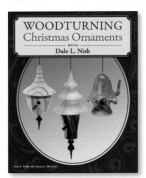

**Woodturning Christmas
Ornaments with Dale L. Nish**
ISBN 978-1-56523-726-1 **$22.99**

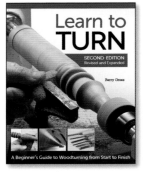

**Learn to Turn, 2nd Edition
Revised and Expanded**
ISBN 978-1-56523-764-3 **$19.99**

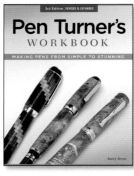

**Pen Turner's Workbook, 3rd
Edition Revised and Expanded**
ISBN 978-1-56523-763-6 **$19.99**

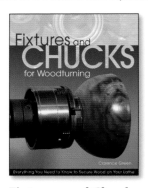

**Fixtures and Chucks
for Woodturning**
ISBN 978-1-56523-519-9 **$22.95**

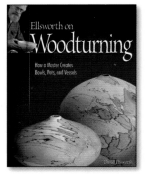

Ellsworth on Woodturning
ISBN 978-1-56523-377-5 **$29.95**

The Frugal Woodturner
ISBN 978-1-56523-434-5 **$19.95**

New Masters of Woodturning
ISBN 978-1-56523-334-8 **$29.95**